pj flaming

voir dire
Copyright © 1994 by pj flaming

Several of these poems have been previously published in *BOA, Downtown Eastside Newsletter, New Muse of Contempt* and *sub-Terrain* magazines.

No part of this publication may be reproduced, sorted in a retrieval system or transmitted, in any form or by any means, without the prior written permission of the publisher or, in the case of photocopying or other reprographic copying, a licence from the Canadian Copyright Licensing Agency (CANOPY), 6 Adelaide St East Suite 900, Toronto ON M5C 1H6. Ph (416) 868-1620, 1-800-893-5777.

New Muse is an annual manuscript award for unpublished poets administered by M·A·P·Productions.

Author photo by Patricia Schneider.
Design by Joe Blades

First edition
Printed and bound in Canada by Sentinel Printing, Yarmouth, N.S.
10 9 8 7 6 5 4 3 2 1

Canadian Cataloguing in Publication Data
Flaming, P. J.

    Voir dire

    (New Muse ; 1994)

    Poems.
    ISBN 0-921411-26-X

I. Title. II. Series.

PS8561.L46V65 1994   C811.'54   C94-950229-4
PR9199.3.F54V65 1994

Broken Jaw Press
BOX 596 STN A
FREDERICTON NB E3B 5A6
CANADA

voir dire

pj flaming

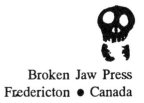

Broken Jaw Press
Fredericton • Canada

voir dire

Introduction   9

breakfast poems

In Search of the Breakfast Special (1990)	12
Lost cars miles & loves (1993)	13
Men in Cars (1992)	17
My Friends (Spring '89—Haida Gwai Poetry Tour) (1989)	18
The unmarked grave of the earmarked wage slave (1989)	21
The wonderful world of advertising...or... What's wrong with this picture? (1993)	23
Listen *.ist! (1992)	27
I hate the Left (1992)	29

bedtime poems

Betrayal (1990)	31
"this is not a love song" (1989)	32
After all (1992)	35
Forever (1992)	36
swimming hole (1992)	37
s/mothering tongues (1987)	38
new couple (1990)	39
separation on the half shell (1992)	40
venus on the half curl (1993)	41
old world new love (1994)	42
old love (1993)	43

place poems

The North
Clearcut (1989)	45
Away (1989)	46
Snow Fall (1989)	47
endless days & northern lights (1989)	49
Emotional abyss/abacus (1989)	50
faulkner n' freddy n' me (1989)	51
August home (1989)	52

other places
Flamingo field (1993)	54
Lava dust (1992)	55
otavalo is not in ecuador (1993)	59

big city
early rising in strathcona (1989)	62
Big City Lonely (1991)	63
Big City Sex & Violence (1990)	65
Strathcona park on Sunday morning (1989)	66

alberta
Town of Canmore (1990)	68
The valley (1990)	69
Home home on the range (1990)	70
family tree (1990)	72
Elements of style (1990)	73
Drive to canmore (1991)	75
Home (1993)	76

● ● ●

Afterward, by Joe Blades — 78

Introduction

Poets have no corner on the market of truth
(one womyn's truth is certainly most men's poison)
Poetry is the uncensored voice

In daily life   we compromise continuously   for whatever reasons
not to offend   to make gains   to flatter
Compromise is the essence of "good" communication

Poetry is the unleashed voice navigated by external circumstance
& experience
It is where we speak free and true

Poets are not endowed with any special gifts
We are not shamans or high priests
We are ordinary people who speak our mind's eye and our heart's tongue

Poems and their poetry have their own logic and time frame
Some poems speak from "I" and some poems from "i"—
belying a diversity of voices
The *voir dire* poems span a period of seven years
and several more life phases
The context of the poetry is defined by the experience of the times
The poetic voices always changing
They are *all* angry poems   Funny poems   Love poems

I welcome you to my journeys here
I encourage people to read my poems out loud
I am a performing poet
There is a lot of rhythm in this stuff
These are not stuffy scholarly works to be read behind bookshelves
These are poems that want to be heard—so speak   yell
shout more truth speak! more *voir dire*!

pj flaming
1993

breakfast poems

In Search of the Breakfast Special

I shoulda known better than to wander off on yesterday's turf
I keep trying to forget that they are taking away *my* city
I mourn
The Sportsman's Cafe is gone
I rage
at the peachy keen yuck all over the place

Where is *my* city?
What have they done to *my* town?
Where have all the All Day Breakfast Specials gone?

Everything is super lite
or high fiber
or French pastry
or bran muffin

I don't want to taste a smoke-free environment
I just want my good old breakfast special—
2 eggs on brown
a side a hash
and the kind of coffee
that makes you spit and go
"Pppsslllllsttt!
What you call this?   coffee?"

Where you slide into a yellow vinyl booth with a faded beige arborite table and drink free refill after free refill from a waitress with a cigarette dangling from her mouth   her ashes sprinkling yer sunnyside ups

Where you can read the paper from front to back   do the crossword puzzle   and even write this poem on the napkin

I just about give up on my search for the All Day Breakfast Special
when I round a corner and there it is   hanging there
in a streaky greasy window—an old cardboard hand written sign
"All Day Breakfast Special 1.99"

Hanging there like a breath of good ol' fashion stale air

Lost cars miles & loves

In loving memory

I still double check to see if that's you behind the wheel and those shades
whenever I see a grey '82 Toyota Celica drive by   I've spent my whole
life looking for you and your cars

From the dark brown '68 Parisienne
to the royal blue '69 Dodge hardtop
to the sandstone '66 Buick Le Sabre
to the black '68 VW
to the aquamarine '64 American Rambler
to the green '72 Volvo wagon
and finally—the grey '82 Toyota Celica

All older functional cars with just the slightest arrogance of style
that comes from being downwardly-mobile but never without class

We made love in all of them
In the Parisienne
the Dodge
the Buick
the VW
the Rambler
the Volvo
and even the compact Toyota

In the front seats
the back seats
the bucket seats
the pullman seats
between the seats
on the hood
alongside the doors
standing up
reclining
bending
rolling
driving

We explored our first fondlings and every conceivable ecstasy in the Parisienne and the Dodge   The shadow of your parents' ownership gleefully punctured between our hard youth night after night   Marijuana seeds and come lining the cracks of the upholstery as your dad drove to work the next day

We covered a lot of miles   in more ways than one   We gave more than one semi-truck driver a cheap thrill as he passed us on the highway looking down into naked driving sex as casual as the labour you do for a living

The Sabre was your first real very own car   Bought from Ian Skeet down the street   Son of a mechanic   You got a deal because he always had a crush on me   We hopped in and drove all the way to Bragg Creek making it on the river bank   sprawling happy bums and breasts tingling with sunburn and a kind of forever feelin' okay

You inherited the VW from your brother   In Calgary siblings' cars are like old alpaca sweaters—you just pass them on to the next in line when you've outgrown them

We packed up the VW and moved our few belongings to Lethbridge in 1979
We tried our hand at
S/M
disco
psychology
and philosophy
but something was missing

Months later   you left me standing on the cooleys in the dead of winter without a ride back to Calgary   just because I had sex with your best friend   Never mind that it was badly done and ill gotten on a drunken New Year's Eve
all because of a misunderstanding about time and place
You treated it like murder in a time when sex was as casual as your brother's hand-me-down sweaters   You said   and you were serious
"I'd kill you if I could get away with it"

But in 1982 you drove that VW all the way out to Vancouver just to be
with me after some gutless little prick attacked me in the middle of the
night half a block from home and left me blinded by my own blood
You wouldn't leave   So we got married

You passed the VW onto your sister and her partner   You were hurt and
disappointed when they sold it for parts a few years later

In 1985 we lived in the "Rambler Motel" as you called it—in between
squats and rented rooms and warehouses   We would ramble around in the
Rambler all day   Me snoozing   with the pullman flat out until 6 pm and
the start of free parking   when we could park the car   stretch our
cramped legs dance all night   get up in the morning   and do it all again
I left you for Montreal   I fell in love with a womyn but the shadow of
you came between us as sure as a stick shift between bucket seats when
you're trying to kiss good night and all   When I flew back to the Coast
a year later   the Rambler was gone but you were still here ready and
waiting it seemed

She followed me out here and fell into bed with someone at the Lotus
Hotel   You and me lived at the Europe Hotel   We didn't need a car   We
couldn't afford to feed it

You didn't get wheels again until the Volvo in 1989—the short-lived
rattletrap you drove me to the organic farm on Horse Lake in   You left to
go tree planting in Barriere without even saying hello to any of the others
It was 40 degrees Celsius out that day   On the way there we stopped in
Merrit   I still have the warm cow-skin fleece vest you bought me for a
dollar   You always had a knack for second hand kitsch retro and planning
ahead for stormy weather

Finally   in the fall of 1989   your mother gave you the '82 Toyota
that she'd been promising you since 1984—dangling it in front of you like
a reconditioned carrot in mint condition   Your first and last cars attached
by strings to your parents' purse and hearts   They buy your love and keep
you in place & comfort in their False Creek condo   And you had the gall
to complain about the noise in *my* neighbourhood where I was struggling
to pay the rent   You tried to chisel me down for the time you spent there

We didn't speak for months   The day the divorce came through   you
called me up and asked me to go for a drive   You were homeless and

jobless   We ended up driving all over BC   the Toyota smooth handling all the way down to Portland and Long Beach

We had a little fun but mostly it was over a long time ago   I wondered what got into you
A high-octane mix of booze
spiked with angst anger
and redneck ways
You were just an asshole
To everybody

It feels like I spent my whole life looking for you and your cars
Fucking fighting living touring riding in your cars   The only thing you could do for me that I couldn't do for myself
drive me here
drive me there
and never forgetting to remind me about it

I'm finally ready for my own   It's someone else's turn to double check
to see if that's me behind the wheel and those shades whenever I drive by

Men in Cars

Men in cars
watch me walk
talking to myself
out loud

A poem pops
outta my mouth
full blown
Instamatic like
a Polaroid snapshot

Men in cars
slow down
They think I am fair game
(mad muttering alone)
And I am
Fair game

I won't leave them
gutted and gasping
disembowelled
from the inside out
their hearts and spirits
smashed forever
as they lurch through life
from safety shelter
to bomb shelter

I am
fair game
I only shoot to kill

My Friends (Spring '89—Haida Gwai Poetry Tour)

my friends are all afloat
washing up
to rest on my beach
rare and delightful as
japanese glass floaters
on Haida shores

my friends are all used up
migrant workers in the industries
planting plugs or picking fruit
when they would rather be
painting paintings
or scratching lines
"artists gotta make a living too"
they say   shaking their heads
wondering how much longer
their knees or backs will hold out—
hazards of the industry
as age encroaches
like pro athletes
workers' shelf–lives are
"nasty   brutish & short"
and not nearly as well–paid

my friends are all confused
uncertain reticent sorts
unable to make decisions
about basic living
let alone "careers"
working and eating
in fits and starts
as the industry demands it

we question
too much
too often

our all night talks
scrape away the idealism
down to the barebones of horror
at the system
and our inability
to make a difference
leaving us with
fewer answers than hangovers

my friends are all diverse
like a rich and textured
ecosystem our diversity
keeps us somewhat stable
finding homeostasis in a world
that is crashing into oblivion
and defying all universal truths

my friends are invisibly webbed
in el salvador
montreal   new york
banff   vancouver   europe
japan   keremeos
wherever we happen to be
at whatever particular time
we are unrelenting wanderers
addicted to motion
and the desire to see

our webbing keeps us warm
our distance keeps us intimate
we fear losing each other
we are too familiar
with the breeding of contempt

my friends are all my family
scattered uncommon oddballs
we have more skeletons in our closets
than we have time or desire to deal with
we prefer to dance & drink & carry on
to celebrate
our occasional occasions   our bad attitudes

my friends are all very loyal
we've been booted around enough
we need each other
we love each other
we tell each other "i love you"

my friends all come to visit
in dream time
we meet
warn
dance
touch
linger & speak
being in dream time is as real to us
as being in your time is real to you

my friends are all adrift
touching base
less often than we need
but whenever we possibly can

The unmarked grave of the earmarked wage slave

Teacher says: Joanie   what do you want to be when you grow up?
Joanie says: Well...I gee...I dunno...I guess I want to be a WAGE
*   SLAVE just like my dear ol' ma*

Come on down
Catch the old wave
We got something
That you crave
Knuckle down and behave

Close the ranks
Sharpen the files
And join the wage slaves!

Lotsa roads we need to pave
Privatization is the rave
Grab a shovel
Don't you shirk
Just get to friggin' work

We've balanced the budget
Don't you fudge it
'Cuz it's wages and welfare that YOU gave
Just so Gillette could make a clean shave
Look himself in the mirror and say
"I liked it so much...I bought the whole country"

Just bite the bullet and be brave
'Cuz ain't no money you gonna save
When you're a wage slave

Don't blame us
Quit makin' a fuss
'Cuz it's jobs and benefits that YOU gave
Come on down
Don't you quiver
'Cuz if you do
We'll just waiver away
Your right to put up a fight

Close the ranks
Sharpen the files
And join the wage slaves

All you ladies
Starve at home and have
lotsa babies
Your free labour
We will savour
If you gals want a job
Don't sit on your pretty butts and sob

Sew some pieces
Serve fast food
The womanly work
will do you good

And if ANY of you all
Dare to dream
That some day you'll
Get some of our cream
Just remember God Supreme
And pray for a place beyond the grave
'Cuz we ain't never ever
And I mean never
Let you be nothin' but a wage slave

Close the ranks
Sharpen the files
And join the wage slaves

The wonderful world of advertising...
or... What's wrong with this picture?

Imagine

"Positive anarchy"
the ad says in corporate punk style
"Bicycle your way to charity"
Imagine what John Lennon and Sid Vicious would think—
"Look what they've done to our song ma"
Never mind Emma and Louise rolling over in their graves
reminding us to dance *and* revolt
but bicycle for charity?

Because the revolution is in—mouthwash?
Masked chuppies (children of yuppies) throw molotov Scope
making the Real Thing (revolution) nothing but a good sales pitch
sold to us for the price of cool breath on a hot date

Benetton gives us united colours with
images of white supremacy
white man's paw encompasses black child's hand
Old Benetton himself flashes it all on centre page
his penis hidden behind the "B"
Bollocks Benetton
Balls Benetton

Coca–Cola is the tribal cultural beat
Glub a glub a glub glub a belch
Choking on the rotten teeth of the children
weaned on Coke or Nestlés
while their mothers breasts are cut off
bursting with the poisons
of the toxic waste dumps
where they work
for the Man in the Coca–Cola plant
for pennies from his Heaven
and the Church and the State
and the corporate bedfellows
have an orgy on our backs

Glub a glub a glub a glub
and white women in the North
get their breasts cut   implanted
colonised for beauty?
Radiate your wrinkles away
Reduce your signs of aging
Reduce your weight
Reduce your income
Reduce your expectations
Reduce your wallet size
Reduce your capacity to think to feel
Reduce at all costs by all means necessary

In 1993 the red sportscar still
comes equipped with the blonde bombshell
Some things just never go out of style
But they tell us we want it that way
We want it that way
Unemployed women
line up for a shot at centrefold
Oh yes   Every girl dreams to have
her picture masturbated on by
disgusting men   Aim high boys
But girls   keep your knickers and your hopes down
And remember   You want it that way
Be nice be nice be nice
Barbie always has lots of nice things
Who buys them for her?
Barbie shore don't work for a living
Must be Ken doll   Or Sugar Daddy doll

Anacin proves the theory
that First Nations people really are
our worst headaches and "mine too"
agrees the smiling young womyn
Her red power reaching
for the bottle of white pills
"They need white people
to look after them"
All this in 30 seconds
Very sophisticated genocide

American Express
"Don't leave home without it"
especially if you have a country to invade
It makes the night life smooth
after a long rough day
of bombing plundering and killing children
But ya get yer worker's compensation
in the bottom of a bottle
Beer is no longer good enough
to keep the workers pissed
—let them drink Caesars
it's the closest they'll ever get to power

At home the boys play
war games in uniforms
with baseball bats and hockey sticks
and the children Nintendo their way
to the future of annihilation

And 50 cents a week
buys a kid off the street
A pimp is a pimp
even from the comfort of your living room
Put yourself in *that* picture

Now IS the time for Positive Anarchy
as if there were any other kind
—the liberation of all peoples from
corporate government colonial control
over our de mock racy
Spoonfeeding us lies
through their televisions
and newspapers we are forced to buy
in the illusion of multiple choice
The Voice is the same
The Wizard is not our friend
And this sure ain't Kansas
or Kahtsalano or Squamish or Lillwat
or no place no more
Clicking our heels and smiling nicely
only means we die with smiles on our faces

We want to truly unite all colours
to reclaim all our lands   all our lives
to stand firm
in the grassroots of the
tribal culture that beats
in our mother/warrior breasts
to radiate reduce and drive all
signs of raging away
to regain calm community
to touch   to become our dreams

You are dead
You are dying
Benetton and Southam
and Thompson and Pattison and
every other goddamn white rich man's son
You are dead

Unmask the voices of revolution in our hearts and mouths
and you'll never leave home again—with or without it
'Cuz my molotov
just bicycled its way to your charity
and gave all the money and land back to where it came from
My sisters and brothers and all the little children of the world

Imagine

Listen *.ist!

(never say i told you so but i told you so)

Your dogma
done caught up with
my catma
Done run
in my
red stocking
Done do me in
between the
skin of
our teeth
Between the sheets of
your body politic
Under the lies of
your delusion
of unity
of your
di-vision of lunacy
your diminishin' democracy

Hah!   We knew all along
that fascism been here
been tapping our phones
been following us home
been putting us in jail
been blowing the bail
been holding AK-47s to our
pretty little heads
been burning our bridges
been busting our circles
been calling us radicals anarchists and *.ists

But when we came to you
with blood on our hands
with death in our ranks
with fear in our homes
with friends in the jails
You just rolled your
social democratic eyes
and told us to vote for
the right Left party

Hey *.ists!
Glad you waking up
to the Big Picture
but we been talking
global control
imperialism
death squads
democracy
What?
Democracy
Where?
You talk about the end of it
We never seen the beginning of it
Are you just slow learners
or tone deaf to the
music of the revolution?
We been talking it
drumming it
banging it out
long before
you were even allowed
to vote

And we don't
sell our souls to
no party
no time
no where
dig?

(*fill in the blank with social– commun– lenin– marx– femin– reform–)

I Hate the Left

I hate the Left
but the Right
is worst

bedtime poems

Betrayal

What is friendship
if not a backdoor
to the bedroom
a welcome mat
to the bed?

"this is not a love song"
—Johnny Lydon

"this is not a love song"
'cuz we passed thru that phase
when the singer was still Rotten

kids teens twenties thirties
we did all the things
we really shouldn't
rebelled & rampaged
our way through a few
rites of passage
made null & void

we kicked the ladder over
scuttled like roaches
sidewinded like snakes
crawled like drunks
helixed spiralled &
gone plain outta control

we tented squatted rented
we fucked married separated divorced
(not necessarily in that order)
we climbed   we strolled
we built
broke down
and built some more

all traditions re-invented from
the eye of our storm
we've passed the test of...
but who's counting?
to everyone else I want to spit
"kids... novices"
because only time will fell
the illusion that time
will tell anything at all
but miles & cross-country smiles
& continental divides
that stand in good stead my friend

only you & me can
remember when
sharing our secrets

the link is not sealed
in diamond or stone
like all nuclear families we react
to fission fusion futures
& possible paths
because of the many ways we walk
is there a universe able to contain the clash?
is it inevitable?   our meeting
again and again
the rupturing disembowelling
molecular meltdown

keirkegaard spoke true
not just either/or
but so many outsiders
people from away
want us bound in
their fantasies of reality
occasionally we defer
risking complete madness

but mostly
we live where we live
the way that we live
struggling to survive
that's all mate
nothin' fancy
certainly not the stuff of *belle lettres*
just ballpoint pens & scratch pads
to battle the monsters of obstruction
the conspiracies of all things real or not
and to you this will all make sense
Now that's a buddy

After all

After all is said and done
There is nothing more to say

Even these cliches
are pressed out of me
flat   stiff   dry
Insignificant
as the cardboard liner
in the crown of your ballcap

Forever

Forever   bound me to you
like morning glory
clinging   to the wall of our house

Pushing   through the cracks
of the foundation
intractable   and there to stay

Forever   dead
Forever   gone

I hope you really mean it   this time

Swimming hole

Dedicated to Patricia

It hurts so bad
  (but you will never tell)
just saying so
  heaps insult onto injury
already beyond repair
  Way down deep   below your
cold calm
          surfaces
like rising eddies
   in the swimming hole
ready and waiting
         to drown you

Your pain
  (like your paintings and photographs)
looks away from the viewer
at something   off canvas
  off camera

Beyond the eye of the beholder
 averted   restrained
  only a flash
of the spreading groundfire
   in your ebony eye

Sometimes you are
   brittle as the bones
carrying the heavy hollow burden
   rounding your thin thin shoulders

s/mothering tongues

having little left
but the illusion
of our bond
    age
you massacred
even this

searching for
pen and notebook
the tools for
rendering it
real

you grab my wrist
you stop my blood flow

"oh leave me alone"
leave me alone
leaving me alone

my touch
lost
in your tongue
my man my man
my man
all man
don't matter
who man

my woo myn
touch
is lost
on your tongue

new couple

the new couple
                      float by
                    wrapped in
          hermetically-sealed logic
while i
      swim
around
        like
             "a fish
             without a
             bicycle"

d
 r
  o
   w
    n
     i
      n
       g

                in the alien
                blood of
                their bubble
                headed universe

the crazy lady
wielding a pick axe
picking away
at the rocks
in your head
the lies in
your bed

i can't seehearsmelltouch
her truth   smug & seamless
                                    covergirl commercial

separation on the half shell

Separating our lives is
   splitting atoms
electrons from photons
   splicing genes
DNA from RNA
   creating creatures
mutating new cells/selves
   wrenching from umbilicus
breaking bonds
    never meant   to be broken

Abstracted from our   life/mates
In spirit we are wanderers
In essence we are gibbons   monogamous
for all our known lives   and then some

Splintered now   like the core of a eucalyptus tree
struck down by lightning   The sweetness bleeds out
of our naked centres and hardens in the wind

venus on the half curl

one hand half curled
            around her soft belly
the other half curled
        around my breast
my heart half curled
     around you
the other half curled
   around me

old world   new love

in between music & maps lies magic
knowing you know these things
back of my back   hands like shovels
digging out new geography
land where nothing
stops friction
heat in afternoon
between sheets   under cover
contour lines   sweat
rolling down spines
notes from a broken jig sliding
into clef of my curve
(the one you don't have)
in kilt and light i could
roll you up   play you
sheet music from *my* world
("Harvest Moon" not "Harvest Home")
mount you   ridges from *my* range
(Rockies not Highlands)
ritual rhythm   steady gait
celtic reel   sheer scale
certainty in what you do   you do do well
again   again   again
navigating (soundtrack of my) instrument
fine tuning (panorama of my) instrument
playing desire   accordion on fire
charting need cartographer
making new views (out of old worlds)
reflect far beyond
shadow/s of (y)our (lovely) gaze

old love

enraptured by quixotic
                chaotic
     obsessions past

a love affair
unable to peel myself away
        passionately glued to
   hollow offerings

i wallow in the airs
of ancient history
present and prescient
as swelling flesh

while the moon waxes full
as a broad bellied woman
bathing in an ice cold river
my love for you wanes

place poems

The North

Clearcut

Clearcut   from Squamish to Prince George
Clearcut   from Nanaimo to Bella Bella
Clearcut   Final solution
It's very clearcut
Clearcut   Clear out of British Columbia

When i see our earth
   all battered & bruised
& ruptured & scarred
   & torched & raped
i see that she is a woman after all

Away

Away from personal & political ambitions
Away from box housing & noisy drunks & mean streets & chipped shoulders
Away from constant urban struggle & all out societal assault
Away from neuroses & sociological pathos
Away from thin walls & cockroaches & manic depressions
Away from very particular horrors
Away away away
There is a way
To go!

Having few expectations
Just beauty
Just mountains
Just away
Getting so much more

Snow Fall

To the top of the King's Throne   we climb
Along the ridge   we walk straight into the St Elias Range
Snow capped peaks meld into infinity
So large that my cherished Rockies look like goosebumps
I see whole   anew
Being Alive has its moments
Tears stream down my cheeks
Breath catches in my chest

     Mountains move hypnotically
        Mountain goats
            traverse trails
    Above multitudinous lakes circs & tarns

We start to descend
I test a snow chute for glissading   I trip and tumble down the ice
        Rolling rolling rolling   somersaulting
            like a dummy in a stunt movie
Trying hard to pitch in
    with my willow walking stick
Heading   straight
   for
   the
   rocks
   a hundred
metres below

Hitting   terminal velocity
Flipping   up in the air a full 360
Digging   my heels into the rocks
Landing   face first in the scree
Dredging   a new waterway with my elbows
          a new carve in the erosionary path

Coming out with only a few scrapes and bruises
More shaken than hurt
My companions more terrified than me
Stopped dead in the scree

We pick our way slowly down the north face
The mountain blasts us with occasional small boulders
Reminding us who is King

Feeling foolish   more certain than ever
Being Alive
is better than
Being Dead

There must be easier ways to remember these basic truths

endless days & northern lights

Meteor shower so close so constant
I could reach up and swallow
the speed the heat
of the white fireballs
leaving tails in our minds
while the earth fire smouldered

After three weeks of rain
it cleared the next day
the kind of sun that makes boys and girls
strip off all their clothes
and plunge buck naked into pristine Christine Lake
The proper tourists minding their children
taking sidelong glances at tom's and freddy's and faulk's whatsits

On the ferry southbound we almost dropped on our knees and prayed
to the cathedral prism

```
            blue
  purple            green
red                 yellow
            white

      circle on circle
         on circle
```

"I've worked this ferry run 15 years   and I've never seen anything like it"
Rosie says

I've walked this earth for well over 30   and neither have I

Emotional abyss/abacus

And when i'm with you
i think "what a gem"
what a perfect l'il boy
i think i am fallllllllling in love
with the way you care
clean house cook meals
run errands offer to help
such a gem

And when i bang with him
i think "what an asshole"
too bad his hair curls that way
and his skin is so smooth
i could ride it all the way home
i think i am combatting
lust desire madness
He doesn't do toilets
but he sure keeps my plumbing flushed

faulkner n' freddy n' me

travelling flings
brushes with touch
more deadly than "real life"
steeped more in
fiction & possibility
than fact & fulfilment

the open-ended question of desire unrequited
swirls in the tension
that engulfs us
the slanders the rebuffs
the splicings & mergings

constant banter edged with
misguided unspoken emotion
underlaid with uncertainty
insecurity of ego & personal lines
not knowing where the ground is safe
edging closer
barking each other off like mad dogs
faulkner's brutal desire
to be admired
freddy's passive power
over us
faulkner hugging fucking touching
assumed and comfortable
freddy waiting for permission

August home

starving & in great need
the denouement
the disappointment of
"being home"
the sheer ugliness of reality
hits square on like the wall of rain
backdropping the inevitable realization
of futility   of despair
as i turn my lock in the door
and wipe my feet on the faded welcome mat

place poems

other places

Flamingo field

She had never been to Florida before   Every morning she looked out the window of her little room to see the Miami grey smog dwarfed by the giant flamingo field that glowed like a vision   It was a billboard ad for headache medicine   "Rise above the madding crowd" the ad said as one lone flamingo soared through the two-dimensional air   She would sponge herself and stare at the flamingo field   Florida had the kind of muggy heat that sticks to your skin and entrails and won't wash off no matter how many sponge baths you take   This was Florida   The flamingoes and the muggy heat

The dingy hotel was under one of the cloverleafs that weave Miami together like daisy chains on a tea cosy   It was the cheapest hotel she could find   It was really a place where old folks live   She wasn't old   She was only 19   She stuck out bright and red as the ladybug that landed briefly on her concrete windowsill before flitting away   She wondered where it came from and if it would find some real green grass

She was in Miami for one reason and one reason only   and that was to get out of there   Miami had the cheapest tickets to Merida   The flights only left every few days   She rode all the way to Miami from Ottawa in 31 hours in a VW bug with two students   The students   a couple   were on spring break from studying anthropology   They asked her why she wanted to go to South America alone   She just shrugged   The couple exchanged knowing looks   She sighed and snuggled up in the backseat with the memory of her trip across Canada   a snow white pillow to rest her fears on

They ate Easter breakfast in Savannah Georgia   The waitress had hair and lips as fake and sweet looking as a jar of maraschino cherries   Her long thin nose propped up her rhinestone cats' eyes glasses   "Throw some more grits on the griddle" she hollered in her made for TV Southern drawl   This was Georgia   Grits and sassy redheads

She caught the plane to Merida that night   She could see the lone flamingo rising above the madding crowd from the window of the plane   She was on her way South   By herself   She had never been to Mexico before

Lava Dust

On the volcano

High up on the slopes of an old volcano in the dust dry mountains of Ecuador a lone campesino stakes out a farm

Clinnng

Clinnng

Clinnng

His hoe rings out hitting the hard lava rock

Clinnng

Clinnng

Clinnng

The singular sound resonates like a giant tuning fork bouncing from the lava rock through the stone dead air to the rounded walls of the broad crater and back again   The campesino's nostrils flare thick with lava dust

Round the curve of the crater the gringita tumbles down the powdery grey slopes   She tosses a lava rock into the water of the crater lake
"It floats!"   she shouts   Breaking the monotony

Clinnng

Clinnng

Clinnng

Punctuating the cacao quechuan silence with her white English noise
Colouring   the lava dusted slopes with her market bought juipile
Covering   her thin shoulders with long blonde hair
Piercing   the flat sky with her bright blue eyes

Young and wiry like a boy
Slim and small breasted
Fit   from basic living on the road

Clinnng

Clinnng

Clinnng

"How can he farm on lava dust?"   she asks   Knowing that the answer lies in the fincas of the landowners sprawling in the lush lands far below
Campesinos pushed to the highest heights
Pushed to where the land is no good for growing
No good for life

Clinnng

Clinnng

Clinnng

At the Hacienda

"Venga   venga gringita y gringo   Bienvenidos a mi hacienda"
The finca senor leers through yellow teeth   "Hacienda Rrrrrrrica"
He rolls his "r"s like a busker selling fruit in the marketplace   "rrrico rrrrico rrrico!"   He rolls up the electronic window of his black shiny car and pulls in the driveway under giant archways   Hacienda Rica
On the edge of the road   Outside Banos   On the way to the jungle

Senor barks out sharp commands
"Asiete"   They sit on bamboo and jaguar skin
"Come"   They feast on luscious fruits and meat
"I am a rich man no?"   His accent is thick like his eyebrows   They nod
"Mira"   They stare at the view from the verandah

Waxy broadleafed trees
Fleshy fruits swing from the limbs
Ripe and ready to pick
Campesinos sweat in white hats and open shirts

Chop

Chop

Chop

Machetes chop hard at the roots

"Bebe"
They drink guava mate   Thick and numbing   Strong as heroin
"Si si Gracias senor"   Gringita grasps the large vaso with her small thin hands   Senor turns up the flamenco music on his sensurround stereo
He is proud   Proud of his rich house   Of his big land   Of his modern life

Gringo stumbles to the bano and wretches out the avocadoes   the meat   the mate   He wretches until there is no more

Senor grabs young gringita   Very fast   Very smooth for such an old man   Gringita wretches at his hands on her breasts   on her bum   His hands clutch and tear

"Ahhh chiquitaaaaaaa"   he moans as if he would break from the mere thought of himself with his hands all over her   His cock hard   Ugly   Bulges under polyester pants   "Cheap pants for a rich man"   she muses

Chop

Chop

Chop

The bright red blossoms   out of the bland beige   fresh and unforgiving

On the Volcano

Cling

Cling

Cling

Her lips are dried and split   The hot wind blows lava dust
It stings her eyes and face   She climbs back up the rim of the volcano

Cling

Cling

Cling

The campesino's hoe is relentless   The lava dust settles where there is no life   And clings to the edge of the volcano

otavalo is not in ecuador

otavalo is not in ecuador
it is tucked quietly between
my corazon and hypothalamus

otavalo is not in ecuador
it is further away
untouched by human greed

otavalo is not in ecuador
it is in my dream to live again
in the adobe house
with my neighbours giggling at the guapo
washing clothes on the rocks at the lake when the wind is up
the women   in wraps and white blusas
the men   in hats and black braids
whispering in magic tongues of
spanish quechuan bond & body
"port ti gringita"
"quazagonagitchu"

otavalo is not in ecuador
it is in my feet that shuffle
around the fire in the night
wrapped in the musica of the pipes
smiles hanging in the black night like white snakes

otavalo is not in ecuador
it is in my shoulders where
I carry water on a stick every day

otavalo is not in ecuador
it is here in my guts
where justice and beauty
breed like lombrices on feces

otavalo is not in ecuador
it is close to becoming
near to being

otavalo is not in ecuador
it is here in my fingertips
and in my need

place poems

big city

early rising in strathcona

Early rising in strathcona
chinese elders
dance to the tune
of unity & universe

While world leaders
create new forms of war & chaos
the wu and the wei
are in hand

Early rising in strathcona
the dawn of a thousand cats
hold kitty council

On every dumpster and doorstep
stretching yawning yowling
"wake up   human race   wake up"

Early rising in strathcona
buildings lean and almost touch
the buffer space—a pillow
for their creaking leaking ramshackle bones

Lurching free of parallel lines
like living breathing trapezoids
giving geometry a whole new language

Early rising in strathcona
a neighbours words ring true
"strathcona is the last gem of vancouver"
it really is you know
it really is

Early rising in strathcona
the lions' manes glow white
the dragon's veins grow red
the digging cranes crow restless

Big City Lonely

Back in Big City Lonely again
I'm hounded
I'm drowneded
by that "old friend"

Big City Lonely howls through my soul
like that old tom cat on this full moon night
Ugly n' loud n' rattlin' around in the garbage cans
Moanin' & groanin'
from somewhere outsida itself

Big City Lonely's real different from
Open Road Lonely
Big City Lonely's everywhere in everybody in Big City
Underlying it all like a foundation on a tumble down house
Like bedrock in a dried up river

Big City Lonely can't be hushed up by a
one night   two night   or ten year stand
Big City Lonely's raw and exposed
leaving you dangling like the roots of a broken tooth in a barroom brawl
the harsh smoke cuttin' through you—cold n' smartin'

Open Road Lonely warms to the touch
A deep and purple magic cloak
fuzzy and friendly as gramma's hand–me–down quilt

Open Road Lonely helps you sleep at night
and determine what's wrong
and determine what's right
You need that Open Road Lonely   Out There

It's what gives ya yer edge on smooth dangers
that don't go bump in the night
but crawl up beside you in the broad daylight

Big City Lonely courts Death—an alluring temptress
riding on the slip of a moon on a hot summer night

But Big City Lonely's no safety at all
It's soft and heavy like quicksand
Dragging you down deep and so weak kneed
any passer-by with an invitin' eye can snag ya
Helpless as a salmon heading upstream
netting only the need and hunger and pain
Bleeding all over like flesh cut artery
spurting   bright red   spasmodic
Unstoppable as Death

Mocking you like the illusion of lost loves found in familiar smells
and pubic hairs piercing unwashed sheets
like used fishhooks in a child's fleshy palm
Big City Lonely makes you wanna pull the trigger
jump off the bridge or at least fuck
strange and undesirable people in
strange and undesirable places
Where you can be sure that
your lovers and friends won't find you
leaving no trace of
Big City Lonely behind

Big City Sex & Violence

Walking along the viaduct
I gotta gun in my hand
I pull the trigger
BANG BANG
Your head snaps back
like whiplash in a rear ender
Your forehead splits
like a cracked windshield
& oozes red ketchuppy stuff
BANG BANG
YOU'RE DEAD

Strathcona park on Sunday morning

Early birds compete with
the worms and the humans
to get the best of the garbage

Children play among
needles and condoms
Do they know that they are poor yet?

place poems

alberta

Town of Canmore

The town of Canmore tips its glass
to Lady MacDonald where vehicles speed
treacherously through the trees

Ah! The quiet of the great Canadian Rockies
the gentle hum of General Motors
the sound of tons of metal passing wind

The valley

The valley is weeping
again   She is tired
again   Her vulva is
rupturing for Man
again

The mine lies dormant
After all these years
He's found a new use for Her
A clubhouse for the future golf course

The valley rolls over
gravely   She is tired
again   She is sore
again   She weeps
again   She will never re-cover

Home   home on the range

Or should i say driving range?
In the heart of the fat of the fire
Here on the home range
they kill the messenger
who dares to be alone
who dares to exercise choice
who dares to take a lover or two
who dares to crack the skulls
who dares to say no to golf
who dares to dream of other ways
who dares to challenge

Home   home on the range
they don't want to know
they aren't even interested
they think i am trying to hurt them
WAKE UP!

Or stay out of my way
While the death of the planet rages on
you lobby for golf courses
You wish for my personal comfort
mistakenly believing that *lack*
of comfort is the problem
that somehow a home on the range
is going to stop the devastation
or better yet
will shut me up

You are wrong
i am right
No monopoly on truth
Just a big piece of it

pow wow pow wow wow
the white men are
driving the range tonight
They think the "greening of amerika"
means golf greens
(fastest growing industry)
Is this ecology or
a private club?

i ain't talking oka either
this is canmore alberta
redneck country
heart of the Rockies

Corporations pull the strings
but the middle class
willingly orchestrate
willingly buy

An enemy
to liberation to freedom
to survival
plugging up the aquifers
with dirty diapers
stripping the earth
for your holes in one

For years i defended the
the possibility of alliance
with the consuming class
"we need them"

Now i spit on you
i despise your collusion
your transparent illusion

You are not our friends
you are the enemy within
exorcise the middle class
eat the rich
that will annihilate the corporation

family tree

my family are laurels
druids dancing in the forest
my family are celts
all first nations people
who worship earth
my family were first
long before the anglos & saxons
my family were the troubadours
minstrels and poets
the family tree say it's so

so who are you?
thieves of the soul
in pursuit of capital
scratching out a living
while the spirit topples
you are not my family

Elements of style

water 1

Squatting to pee in the woods again
Pssssshssshshhhhht!

Oops!
Wet sneakers again

water 2

creek crossing
feet on slippery stone
harsh flat
against instep
balance with limb
and stay put

water 3

lips and throat gone dry
while tears stream down cheeks
the saline does not quench the thirst
for you baby for you

air 1

whiplash in the whirlwind
cats will brave anything for a stroke

air 2

breathing again
deeply hungrily
i need
air!

air
swollen with pollen
culled from the surface
of the waterwaterwater
air
freshfreshfresh
air
a life's supply to
hold me over
just one winter
in the city

air 3

breath on cheek
breath on labia
whhhhhhhhew
you took my breath away
with just one blow

Drive to canmore

On the drive to canmore i only half listen to your stories about tugboats and sea
It is the land that has me spellbound now
Breath in heart resting riding on the gusty winds and snow blown roads
One sharp curve rocks the boat
Out on the ice covered lake i see *your* stories your legacy
Your response to the suitcase we found this morning tattered and bursting
Full of sketches letters drawings heart throbs and mother's "most pleasant memories"

Long before you two ever met
mother was an innocent mooning over Harry James under the wide warm southern alberta skies
You were a gangly young tar before your time
"Because I was big" you say "they thought I was 19"
Tugging the sea up and down the coast from sitka to san francisco

Before i hear the ending   i start to hold the beginning
of memories & mountains & mixed metaphors & even before the lines are w/rote these poems are
my stories
my legacy
to whomever will need to know these things

Home

Home is the empty hollow of the universe   the place no one dares to go alone   the curve of the semicircular canal of the Ear of It All   the place where despair flattens out into being   where crying flows until there are no more tears   only a soft emptiness like the underbelly of a cat

"Home is where the heart is"   a mythical place   a whisper   an unrequited desire
Home lives in your dreams   and visits you past bedtime
Home is maintenance free   but the costs of living are high   no security   no definitive walls   just a down payment from the bottom of your guts

Home is where you are free
"Home free   home free"   hide n' seek fantasy home free
Home is more than a rented house on franklin street in a city on a western coast of a northern country
Home is where you always want to be and never get to go
Home is a mansion in the sky   a backpack on your back   a car you've never driven   a girl you've never fucked
Home is the dreamland of home run   home plate   a homer one two three   you're out
Home is a figment of your virulent imagination
Home is in the soul of every sentient creature
Home is the purr of ursaba
Home is where you want to leave
Home is what you never leave without one
Home is a bottomless pit of past fears lives loves and joys
Home is alive in neon satin brocade and a new paint job
Home is what you'll never have
Home is what your parents have and you'll never get
Home is a place you've never been somewhere in New Mexico or Colorado or Snake River

Afterward

So why did I chose pj flaming and her book, *voir dire*, as the first recipient of the New Muse manuscript award?

Because her poetry has spunk. Because the poet who wrote these poems must also have spunk. Must be brash and nervy. Because neither poet not their poems lie down as if dead or even feeling near death. Because there is vitality and life. When pj flaming, in her introduction, says "I encourage people to read my poems out loud," she means it. These are immediate, in-your-face poems. Poems that speak, sing, shout with the rhythms of the highway, of popular or alternative music, chants, the rhythms of the heart and our emotions, the rhythms of the earth. The poems of pj flaming are poems of our times and our concerns. And, because they are not poems written for the library shelf and the student of literature, because they are poems from the street and the people, poems for the street and the people on the street, I believe they embody the spirit of the new muse. The muse that is alive and is bringing poetry back, where it belongs, in our daily life.

Joe Blades
Publisher

Are you New Muse 1995?

Are you a poet without your first book published? The New Muse award is looking for book-length poetry manuscripts in its annual contest. The New Muse 1995 award-winning author will be offered a publication contract and a cash royalties advance of $100 towards having their book published by Broken Jaw Press/M·A·P·Productions in autumn 1995.

Guidelines:
—Entrants must not have published a first full-size poetry book (minimum of 48 pages literary content).
—Enter poetry manuscripts of 50-60 pages, single-spaced. Individual poems may have been previously published in magazines, anthologies and chapbooks. Typed on 8½ x 11 white paper (may be accompanied by Macintosh or HD Word Perfect diskettes). Title and page number must appear on every page. No simultaneous manuscript submissions.
—Include author name, address, phone numbers, manuscript title, and a literary bio note, on a separate sheet of paper.
—Manuscripts will not be returned. Please retain a copy of your manuscript for your files.
—Please enclose a #10 letter-sized Self-Addressed Envelope with Canadian postage (no USA stamps) or an International Postal Reply Coupon (IRC) from your post office, to receive pre-publication notification of the winner (and please send us any change of address you may have during the contest).
—All entrants will receive a copy of the winning book.
—$15 entry fee. Cheque or money order payable to M·A·P·Productions.
—Deadline: 31 March 1995.

NEW MUSE 1995
M·A·P·PRODUCTIONS
BOX 596 STN A
FREDERICTON NB E3B 5A6
CANADA

More Publications You Should Want

Broken Jaw Chapbooks:
Salvador, A.J. Perry
Drawings by Poet, Beth Jankola
Hawthorn, Arthur Bull; Ruth Bull (illustrator)

Broken Jaw Press:
Chaste Wood, karl wendt
Dark Seasons, Georg Trakl; Robin Skelton (translator)
Poems for Little Cataraqui, Eric Folsom
A Lad From Brantford & other essays, David Adams Richards
voir dire, pj flaming. New Muse 1994 Manuscript Award winner.

New Muse of Contempt
Since 1987, *New Muse of Contempt* has been an international magazine of mail art and literary writing—poetry, visual poetry, essays, reviews—edited and published by Joe Blades. $7/year. ISSN 0840-4747

For a full catalogue, please send to:
Broken Jaw Press
M·A·P·PRODUCTIONS
BOX 596 STN A
FREDERICTON NB E3B 5A6
CANADA